KW-272-714

Clare and the Fair
Two Poems

Come to the Fair

Come to the fair!
Come to the fair!

Ride in a car.

Ride in a chair.

Down to the ground and
up in the air!

Mums, dads and children – everyone's there, flying around with the wind in their hair.

Have a good stare.

You might win a fairy.
You might win a bear.

So come to the fair!
Come to the fair!

Clare! Clare!

"Clare, Clare! Look over there!
Who has spilt cornflakes all over the
chair?

Did you do it, Clare?"

"Oh no," said Clare.
"I didn't do it. It was my bear."

"Clare! Clare! Look over there!

Poor little Mary has jam in her hair!

Did you do it, Clare?"

"Oh no," said Clare.
"I didn't do it. It was my bear."

"Clare! Clare! Look over there!
Jars, tins and packets are everywhere.

Did you do it, Clare?"
"Oh no," said Clare.
"I didn't do it. It was my bear."

"Bear, Bear! Look over there!
Who has been giving the kitten a scare?

Did you do it, Bear?"
"Oh no," said Bear.
"I didn't do it.

It must have been Clare."